The Diamond Sutra

Ancient Wisdom in the Age of Terror

The Diamond Sutra

Ancient Wisdom in the Age of Terror

Edited by

The Reverend John Zen Ko

The Diamond Sutra
Ancient Wisdom in the Age of Terror

Copyright 2009 © by the Reverend John Zen Ko

All rights reserved. No part of this book may be reproduced, stored in a retrieval system, or transmitted by any means, electronic, mechanical, photocopying, recording, or otherwise without written permission from the author.

978-0-578-00629-1

Mindwhispers Publications
www.Mindwhispers.net
910 8th Street
Tularosa, New Mexico 88352

Introduction

On the morning of September 11, 2001, people began the day as any of us would. A young man, who worked as a delivery driver for United Parcel Service, kissed his sleeping wife as he left his home before sunrise to begin his day. An asset manager ate a quick breakfast, kissed his wife and children good-bye, and grabbed his attaché case that contained the documents he needed to close a real estate transaction. A young administrative assistant said good-bye to her cat as she left her small apartment. Her fiancé had promised to take her to an exclusive restaurant for dinner. Perhaps he would give her the diamond ring she dreamed about. A family of five set out for the airport to fly to Disney World for the first vacation they had shared in many years. An older couple went to the airport to fly out-of-town to visit their grandchildren whom they had not seen for a long time. A sales representative boarded an airplane. He anticipated closing a lucrative contract and thought how the commission would enrich the lives if his family.

Inside the office tower, people go about the normal routine of a business day. The United Parcel driver chats with his friend in the mailroom. The young administrative assistant checks her e-mail. A colleague stops by and shares the young woman's excitement about the anticipated evening. The asset manager waits in an anteroom for the meeting with the closers. On the airplane, all is normal.

A man stands up and steps into the aisle. Brandishing a box knife, he hauls a male passenger from his seat and slits his throat. Pandemonium erupts. Others join the man with the knife. Two race up the aisle and barge into the cockpit. They overpower the flight crew. Shocked, the passengers realize that they are the victims of a hijacking. The hijackers threaten the rest of the passengers. Women weep. The children cry. Their mother comforts them. She tries to reassure them that they will be all right. The hijackers will take them to another airport, make demands, and let the passengers go. They will certainly release the children. Fretting and anxious, they nervously await the outcome of their ordeal.

They look out the windows and notice that they are flying low over Manhattan. Ahead lie the twin towers of the World Trade Center. They are fast approaching them. They are flying ever lower. Then the awful thought enters their minds; seconds to go. The passengers are no longer riding an airplane but hurdling aboard a flying bomb toward the twin towers; screams, then the blackness of oblivion. In the tower, the sudden thunder of impact, the burst of orange flame and darkness.

The incident at the World Trade Center continues to haunt our collective psyches. We share the terror of those aboard the airplanes and those trapped in the upper stories of the towers above the flames. What would we do?

Many, if they had time, prayed. For others the events were just too terrifying and came too fast. A Catholic priest I know is the survivor of a plane crash. He was lucky. Someone pulled him from the wreckage as the flames engulfed the cabin. The passenger in the seat beside him perished. After fifty pints of blood and months in the hospital, he survived. He still carries the scars of the accident. He cannot stand for long without shifting his weight from one leg to the other. He wears gloves to protect the delicate scar tissue on his hands. He always thought that in a time of crisis, he would have time to make his peace with God. In the tumbling of the cabin, the noise, screams, and flames, as the airplane broke apart, he found that his only response was to be caught up in the moment. No time to think. No time to pray.

Many of us could encounter tragedies similar to this. We push the thought of them to the back closets of our minds, but the realization that we might face our end in a sudden moment of terror cannot be escaped. Even if we avoid a tragic end, we cannot avoid our ultimate fate. How do we prepare ourselves for this? In the Christian tradition of the West, we tell ourselves that we can look forward to a life with Jesus in Heaven. Often we hear at funerals 'she is in a better place' or 'God has called him home, to be with Him'. We tell ourselves these things, but we wonder. If these myths are true, why do we fight death? Why to we invest billions on medicines and cures that extend life? Wouldn't it be better not to resist death, so that we can be with God? We wrestle with these questions.

On September 11, 2001, the passengers aboard those aircraft found themselves hurdling toward the Twin Towers, and in that instant, met death. They were like a wave that hurdles toward the rockbound coast of New England. The wave spends its life flying over the surface of the ocean. It may be a large magnificent wave, towering above the sea, or she may just be a small insignificant one. Joyfully, she rises up to meet the sun and the sky. She is unaware of her fate. Then, she sees the rocks on the shoreline. She races toward them. With joy the wave crashes against them, recoils and dies. The wave has no fear. She knows that she and the ocean are one. She returns to her true nature which is the water.

We humans are attached to many things, our notion of self, our bodies, our possessions, our families, our jobs. Clinging to them, we miss the point of existence. Our ignorance prevents us from understanding the true nature of things. All things, the universe, stars, planets, people, and insects come into existence, and after a while, we cease to exist. We are like the waves on the ocean, yet we crave meaning in our existence which is the essence of spirituality.

In reality, we are waves. This is verified by the science of quantum physics. All particles are nothing more than very small bundles of energy that are constantly entering our experience and then vanishing into nothingness. We are nothing more than the particles that occupy the space that we call our bodies. We are quite immaterial, mostly empty space, nothing more than a flux of energy. Scientists search for the identity that is ourselves, but to no avail. The electric exchanges in the synapses of our nervous systems give an illusion of a self, but when we look inside our brains, we find nothing that can be described as a mind, no soul resides there.

The fact that you have taken up this little volume indicates that you are searching for a deeper spirituality. If you are a student and are reading this text as an assignment for a class in philosophy or religion, and still cling to the notion of a self, and a world out there filled with other selves and perhaps universal selves, you have my deepest sympathy. Frequently what people read or hear from the lips of university professors or religious scholars about Buddhism casts misconceptions about Buddhist philosophy. As a scholar, you will find the text ponderous, contradictory, and completely absurd. However, if you are one of those fortunate beings that are truly seeking, then you are the most blessed of beings. The fact that you have taken upon yourself to study this text means that you are more than halfway to enlightenment.

People begin spiritual journeys in search of true meaning. A theology professor of mine declared that people are attracted to new religions because they are dissatisfied with their own religion. Missionaries make new converts solely on the premise that "my god works better than your god." Many in the west have become disillusioned by religion. They see the evil that is done in the name of religion; they discover that the ancient myths no longer tell the story of their lives. They seek something new.

About 2600 years ago, Prince Siddhartha Gautama began such a search. He lived a life of luxury in an area that is now in present-day Nepal. His father protected him from every unpleasantness. However, Siddhartha had an insatiable curiosity about the world and would often sneak out of the palace to explore the world around him. On these adventures he saw, for the first time, the sorrows of life; people who were sick, the very old, the dying, and most horrifying of all, he watched as people prepared a body for cremation on a funeral pyre! He realized that the things that provide pleasure in life are fleeting. It is the condition of all people to sicken and die. Then he met a monk who practiced strict asceticism in an effort to escape the cycle of suffering to which he was bound by ignorance and the consequences of his actions (karma). Siddhartha surrendered his princely life and became an ascetic. After years of extreme asceticism, he found that he was no closer to deliverance from the cycle of suffering. He gave up asceticism and sat under a bodhi tree near the present-day Bodhgaya in India. Sitting cross-legged, with his back straight, his head erect, eyes downcast, and his hands folded in his lap, he sat in deep concentration for many days. In this meditation, he experienced the true nature of existence and purified his mind of all ignorance and defilements and perfected all of his good qualities. His mind awakened to the Truth. He experienced the

Most Supreme Enlightenment and became a Buddha which means 'one who has awakened'. He spent the rest of his life teaching others the way to Enlightenment. Frequently, his disciples would gather around him to receive his teachings in the form of Sutras.

The word *sutra* has many roots, but the usual understanding of the term concerns a written text for us to read. When Siddhartha spoke, people who were highly skilled in mnemonics memorized everything that came from his mouth. Like the ancient storytellers of every culture, it was their duty to recite the words of his sermons[1] and lessons and repeat them to all. Four hundred years after the death of the Buddha, these storytellers and other Buddhist scholars held a convocation and put his words to paper (actually the words were put down on palm leaves in ink and bundled together). These Buddhist scholars referred to them as *The Words of the Lord Siddhartha* and gave each a different name for easy reference. They were referred to as *suttas* or *sutras*. Few of them are attributed to the Lord Buddha. Most were composed by later Bodhisattvas or temple priests. A sutra that begins with the words "Thus I have heard..." or similar words are usually considered to be authentic, being from the author to whom they are attributed.

The Diamond Sutra is one of the oldest and most valued works among the Buddhist Scriptures. To remove the *Sutra* from the Buddhist canon would be equivalent to removing the Letter to the Romans from the Christian New Testament. Upon hearing the *Sutra* recited, the Sixth Zen Patriarch, Hui-Neng (617—713 CE), experienced immediate enlightenment. He went on to write his own commentary on *The Diamond Sutra* which is often referred to as *The Platform Sutra*. *The Diamond Sutra* best describes the Dharma or Buddhist practice. Many translators describe the Dharma as Law, but this is very inaccurate from a Buddhist point-of-view. Buddhists have scriptures, many libraries full of them, but unlike other religions, these scriptures have no authority. There is no Buddhist dogma. There is only Buddhist practice. Indeed, the only authority in Buddhism is the individual. Persons who wish to practice Buddhism attach themselves to a teacher who points the way. There is no obligation to actually search for the way, and the disciple chooses to follow the teacher or not. There is

---

[1] Teisho

no 'hell' or 'heaven' awaiting the disciple who does not follow the teacher's instructions, only the missed opportunity to experience enlightenment. Enlightenment is self-verifying and confirmed by the supervision of the teacher. That being said, *The Diamond Sutra* is the quintessence of Buddhism. To study and practice this sutra is to lead oneself away from such concepts of self, a world out there that is different from ourselves, and universal selves which we often describe as gods. It leads us to the very heart of Buddhism. It is like a threshold that we cross to step out into the wider world of enlightenment. It is the grand Truth with infinite beauty.

Many translations of *The Diamond Sutra* have been published in the English language, but most are by Westerners who have little understanding of Buddhist thought. Many are filled with useless footnotes that try to explain Buddhist teachings in terms of the dualistic sayings of Jesus, Sigmund Freud, Carl Jung, or other Western philosophers. I believe that *The Diamond Sutra* speaks for itself and needs no interpretation. Other translations seek to abridge the text and to remove repetitious phrasing. This does the reader a disservice because they remove one feature of the text that is most endearing. The reader must bear in mind that before the Diamond Sutra was written down, it existed in oral tradition, passed on by word of mouth from generation to generation. The repetitious formulas are mnemonic devices to aid in memorizing the text. I have limited my footnotes to indicating the Sanskrit words that the English words translate. I do this only for those scholars who might take up this little volume. Several translations attempt to rearrange the order of the various stanzas in the text in an effort to find greater clarity. I have moved two stanzas to the end of the Sutra: the one where Subhuti awakens to enlightenment and the other where he asks the Lord Buddha the name by which this sutra will be called. My rationale for this is clear, at least for me. The end of the Sutra seems the logical place for Subhuti to experience enlightenment and then, to ask for the name of the Sutra. There may be good arguments why certain stanza should be moved or should remain in their traditional place, but in my reading of the Sutra, the changes seem to make little difference. My only purpose here is to present *The Diamond Sutra* in a way that is clear and easily understood. My presentation of *The*

Diamond Sutra follows the translations of Max Müller, William Gemmell, and Dwight Goddard.

It is not my purpose here to give an explanation of Buddhist teaching; there is abundant literature on that. I have provided a glossary to explain the meanings of some of the words used in the Sanskrit and Chinese texts. My fervent wish is that someone may find true peace and certainty from reading, meditating upon, and practicing what these pages contain.

The Reverend John Zen Ko
Zen Buddhist Priest
Dharma Mountain Zendo
Cloudcroft, New Mexico
January, 2009

The Diamond Sutra

I have heard this about the Lord Buddha: On one important occasion, the Lord Buddha stayed in the kingdom of Shravasti where he lived in a grove belonging to King Jeta. The grove was within the royal domain which Jeta, the heir-apparent, gave to Sutana, a kind and generous Minister of State revered for his liberal gifts to charity.

Twelve hundred and fifty of his most devout disciples had gathered there, all of whom had attained high degrees of spiritual wisdom.

At the hour of the morning meal, the Lord Buddha, the Honored of the Worlds, dressed himself in the mendicant's attire, and carrying a begging bowl, he entered Shravasti, a great city, to beg for food. He went from door to door and accepted any donations that many of the people thought best to provide. When he finished this religious exercise, he returned to Jeta's grove and ate this meager meal which he received as a gift from the people. After he had finished his meal, he took off his mendicant's robe, laid aside his begging bowl, and washed his sacred feet. Then he took the seat of honor that his disciples had reserved for him.

Then the venerable Subhuti, who occupied a place in the midst of the assembly, rose from his seat. He arranged his cloak so that his right shoulder was bare, knelt on his right knee, pressing the palms of his hands together, and bowed in respect toward the Lord Buddha.

"Honored of the Worlds," he said. "You are the perfection of knowledge about the nature of all things.[2] With amazing awareness, you protect the Faith and instruct this distinguished assembly of enlightened disciples[3]. Honored of the Worlds, if good disciples, whether men or women, seek to obtain the Most Supreme Enlightenment,[4] what should they do to quiet their drifting minds and bring every excessive desire under control."

The Lord Buddha replied to Subhuti: "This is truly an excellent subject. As you say, I protect the Faith and instruct this distinguished assembly of enlightened disciples. Listen carefully to me and I will answer your question so that you and this distinguished assembly of enlightened disciples will understand, and that whenever good disciples, whether men or women, seek to obtain supreme wisdom[5] they simply have to follow what I am about to say to you and they will be able to quiet their drifting

---

[2] Tathagata—frequently used when the Buddha is referring to himself
[3] Bodhisattvas
[4] Anuttara-samyak-sambodhi
[5] Prajna-paramita

minds and bring every excessive desire under control and will be able to attain perfect tranquility."

Subhuti was very pleased at this and asked the Lord Buddha to proceed and the Lord Buddha, in his splendid body and with perfect speech, proceeded to dictate the message of this Scripture.

"Everyone in the world, including the most enlightened disciples, should seek the Wisdom that will enable them to quieten their drifting minds and to bring under control every excessive desire; whether they have been hatched from eggs, formed in the womb, arose by spontaneous generation, or produced by metamorphosis, with or without form or intelligence, with or without natural instinct, and finally awaken to complete Nirvana. Even though the number of sentient beings delivered by this Wisdom is infinite, in reality there are no sentient beings to be delivered. Any disciple who clings to the subjective illusions of form or sensual experiences such as self, personality, other selves, or an eternal Universal Self is unworthy to be called an enlightened disciple.

"Likewise, Subhuti, before the enlightened disciples teach this Wisdom[6] to others, they should free themselves from all cravings brought by beautiful sights, pleasant sounds, delightful fragrances, sweet tastes, gentle touch, and seductive thoughts. In the practice of charity, they should not be influenced by any of these sensual experiences because when they practice charity uninfluenced by such things, they will realize enormous and immeasurable merit.

---

[6] Dharma

"What do you think, Subhuti: Is it possible to estimate the space from one end of the universe to the other?"

Subhuti replied: "Honored of the Worlds, it is impossible to estimate the space from one end of the universe to the other."

"Subhuti, it is equally impossible to estimate the blessings and merit an enlightened disciple will receive who exercises charity undisturbed by seductive sensual experiences. This truth should be taught to everybody."

The Lord Buddha asked Subhuti: "What do you think? Is it possible that by means of his physical body, the Lord Buddha may be clearly perceived?"

Subhuti replied: "No, Honored of the Worlds, it is impossible to perceive the Lord Buddha by his physical body because what we refer to as the Lord Buddha's physical body is not really a physical body."

The Lord Buddha continued: "Every sensual experience is impermanent and deceptive. When the mind realizes that all sensual experiences are illusionary, the Lord Buddha will then be clearly perceived."

The Lord Buddha asked: "What do you think, Subhuti? Has the Lord Buddha reached the Most Supreme Enlightenment or has he given you such a teaching?"

Subhuti replied: "Honored of the Worlds, as I understand the teaching of the Lord Buddha, there is no such thing as the Most Supreme Enlightenment because the teachings of the Lord Buddha are unimaginable and beyond comprehension. They neither exist nor do not exist. They are neither sensual experiences nor things conceived by the mind. This means that Buddhas and enlightened disciples are not enlightened by dogma but by experience that are both sudden and real.

The Lord Buddha asked Subhuti: "What do you think, Subhuti? If a disciple gave alms equal to the seven treasures[7] sufficient to fill the three thousand great universes, would that disciple gain considerable blessing and merit?"

Subhuti replied: "Honored of the Worlds, that disciple would gain very considerable blessing and merit, because what the Lord Buddha refers to as blessing and merit in reality do not contain any objective value or quantity, and in this sense the Lord Buddha only refers to them as having considerable blessing and merit."

The Lord Buddha continued: "If disciples who diligently study and practice just a single stanza of this Scripture and explain its meaning to others, their blessing and merit will be far greater because from these explanations Buddhas have attained the Most Supreme Enlightenment and their teachings are based upon this sacred Scripture, but Subhuti, the words I have used to refer to Buddhas and their teachings have no reality because in reality there are no Buddhas and no teachings.

"What do you think, Subhuti? Could a disciple who has entered into the stream[8] that leads to Nirvana make such subjective assertions as 'I have entered the stream'?"

---

[7] Gold, silver, pearls, coral, cornelian, glass, and crystal
[8] Scrotapatti: Apatti—one who has entered; Scrota—the stream (of holy conduct)

Subhuti replied: "No, Honored of the Worlds. If any disciples were to say that they have entered into the Holy Stream, those disciples have actually not entered anything because disciples who have entered the Holy Stream do not entertain subjective concepts like form, hearing, odor, taste, touch and mental concepts."

Again, the Lord Buddha inquired of Subhuti: "What do you think? Suppose certain disciples have attained such excellence that they are subject to only one more rebirth.[9] Could such a disciple make such subjective assertions as 'I have attained such excellence that I am subject to only one more rebirth'?"

Subhuti replied: "No, Honored of the Worlds. For any disciples to say that they have attained such excellence that they subject to only one more rebirth, they have actually not attained such excellence. Disciples who have attained such excellence know that there is no rebirth in this world or in any other world."

Again, the Lord Buddha inquired of Subhuti: "What do you think? Suppose certain disciples have attained such superior excellence that they are no longer subject to rebirth.[10] Could they make such subjective assertions as 'I have attained such superior excellence that I am no longer subject to rebirth'?"

Subhuti replied: "No, Honored of the Worlds. For any disciples to say that they have attained such superior excellence that they are no longer subject to rebirth have actually not attained such superior excellence. Disciples who have attained such

---

[9] Sakradagami
[10] Anagami

superior excellence do not cling to such subjective concepts as 'I am no longer subject to rebirth'."

Again, the Lord Buddha inquired of Subhuti: "What do you think? Suppose certain disciples have attained the Most Supreme Enlightenment.[11] Could they make such subjective assertions as 'I have attained the Most Supreme Enlightenment'?"

Subhuti replied: "No, Honored of the Worlds. For any disciple to say that they have attained the Most Supreme Enlightenment, they have actually not attained the Most Supreme Enlightenment because disciples who have attained the Most Supreme Enlightenment do not entertain in their minds such subjective concepts as 'I have attained the Most Supreme Enlightenment'. Such ignorant disciples will soon be grasping such things as self, personality, other selves, or an eternal Universal Self. Honored of the Worlds, when you said 'I have attained absolute quiescence of the mind and have reached the very ultimate experience in human attainment and because of it attained the Most Supreme Enlightenment' if your mind had grasped the thought, 'I have attained the Most Supreme Enlightenment and am free of all desire', Lord Buddha, you could not have declared 'Subhuti delights in the practice of silence and tranquility'.[12] Actually, I do not cling to such subjective thoughts, so Lord Buddha; you can truly say that Subhuti delights himself in the practice of silence and tranquility."

---

[11] Arhat
[12] Aranyaka

Again, the Lord Buddha inquired of Subhuti: "What do you think? When the Lord Buddha, in a previous life, was a disciple of the Dipankara Buddha, did he receive any definite teaching or attain any definite degree of discipline that later enabled him to become a Buddha?"

Subhuti replied: "No, Honored of the Worlds. When the Lord Buddha was a disciple of the Dipankara Buddha he truly received no definite teaching nor did he attain any definite excellence that later enabled him to become a Buddha."

Again, the Lord Buddha inquired of Subhuti: "What do you think, Subhuti? Do enlightened disciples enlarge the Buddhist Kingdoms to which they go?"

Subhuti replied: "No, Honored of the Worlds. To use the expression 'enlarge' to describe the Buddhist Kingdoms would be a contradiction in terms, for Buddhist Kingdoms thus enlarged would no longer be called Buddhist Kingdoms. Therefore the expression 'to enlarge the Buddhist Kingdoms' is just a figure of speech."

The Lord Buddha continued to address Subhuti, saying: "All Enlightened Disciples should purify their minds of all concepts that relate to seeing, hearing, tasting, touching and thinking. They should diligently develop their minds to be spontaneous and natural, independent of any preconception arising from the senses."

The Lord Buddha continued to address Subhuti, saying: "Suppose a person had a body as large as Mount Everest, prince among mountains, would that person's body be considered great?"

Subhuti replied: "Exceedingly great, Honored of the Worlds, because when the Lord Buddha refers to a physical body he is not referring to a body that is limited by any subjective concepts that relate to seeing, hearing, tasting, touching, and thinking, so such a body may truly be called 'great'."

Again, the Lord Buddha inquired of Subhuti: "What do you think? If there were as many River Ganges as there are grains of sand in the River Ganges, would the number of these rivers be very great."

Subhuti replied: "Exceedingly great, Honored of the Worlds."

The Lord Buddha continued: "Suppose that these rivers actually existed, how great would be the quantity of sand they would contain. Subhuti, if a good and holy disciple, whether a man or a woman, should give alms equal to the seven treasures for each of those grains of sand, would that disciple's blessing and merit be very great?

Subhuti replied: "Exceedingly great, Honored of the Worlds."

The Lord Buddha continued: "Subhuti, if another disciple diligently studied and practiced one stanza of this Scripture and explained it to another, that disciple's blessing and merit would be far greater. If any disciple, in any place, should teach just one stanza of this Scripture, that place would become Holy Ground and would be held in reverence and would be enriched by the offerings of the gods, immortals, and celestial spirits as though it was a sacred pagoda or temple. How much more sacred would this place be if a disciple studied and practiced all of this Scripture. Be assured, Subhuti, such a disciple will receive spiritual powers equal to attaining the supreme, unsurpassed, and most wonderful Enlightenment,[13] and in the place where this Scripture is reverenced the Lord Buddha and all of his honored disciples will be found."

Again the Lord Buddha addressed Subhuti: "What do you think, Subhuti? Has the Lord Buddha given you any definite doctrine or practice in this Scripture?"

Subhuti replied: "No, Honored of the Worlds, the Lord Buddha has not given us any definite doctrine or practice in this Scripture."

The Lord Buddha continued: "What do you think, Subhuti? Are the grains of dust that fill the three thousand great universes very numerous?"

Subhuti replied: "Yes, Honored of the Worlds, they are very numerous indeed."

The Lord Buddha continued: "Subhuti, when the Lord Buddha refers to 'grains of dust' he does not mean that he has any definite or subjective conception in mind. He merely uses these words as figures of speech. Likewise with the words 'the great universes' do not refer to any definite or subjective concept. They are mere words. Subhuti, if any good and pious disciple, whether a man or a woman, for the sake of charity, has been sacrificing his or her life generation after generation equal to the number of grains of dust in the three thousand great universes, but another disciple has only

---

[13] Anuttara-samyak-sambodhi

been studying and practicing just one stanza of this Scripture and teaching it to others, that disciple's blessing and merit will be much greater."

The Lord Buddha continued: "What do you think, Subhuti? Can the Lord Buddha's personality be grasped by its thirty-two signs of a great man?"[14]

Subhuti replied: "No, Honored of the Worlds, no one can grasp the Lord Buddha's wonderful personality by its thirty-two signs of a great man, because what the Lord Buddha has expressed as 'thirty-two signs of a great man' do not refer to any definite or subjective concepts about the qualities of the Lord Buddha. They are mere words."

The Lord Buddha addressed Subhuti: "What the Lord Buddha referred to as the first and third conditions of Wisdom[15] of Charity and Patience are not really conditions of Wisdom, because in a previous life, the Prince of Kalinga severed the flesh from my limbs and body. At that time, I was free from such subjective concepts of sensual experiences as self, personality, other selves, or an eternal Universal Self. If I had such subjective concepts as self, personality, other selves, or an eternal Universal Self when my limbs and body were torn apart, I would have experienced feelings of anger and hatred.

"In my previous five hundred rebirths, I used life after life to practice patience and humility as though I was some saintly being called upon to suffer, but even then my mind was free from such

---

[14] See the Lakkhana Sutra.
[15] Paramita

subjective concepts of sensual experiences as self, personality, other selves, or an eternal Universal Self. Subhuti, Enlightened Disciples must rid themselves of these subjective concepts of sensual experiences because they are unreal and illusive. When someone aspires to the Most Supreme Enlightenment, their mind should ignore every sensuous influence and remain detached from anything that relates to sight, sound, fragrance, taste, touch, or thought. The Enlightened Disciple cultivates this independence of mind because a mind that is dependent on the external senses is deluded. In reality, there is nothing external to depend on. For this reason, the Lord Buddha has instructed, that in the exercise of charity, the Enlightened Disciple is not to depend on any form of sensual experiences.

"Subhuti, the Enlightened Disciple who wishes to exercise charity should do so, uninfluenced by any preconceived thought regarding the self, other selves, and the intent of helping sentient beings. He is always aware that both sensual experiences and sentient beings are mere expressions. They are ephemeral and illusory. Subhuti, the teachings of the Lord Buddha are true, credible, and unchanging. They are neither extravagant nor the result of my imagination. Subhuti, the level of thought attained by the Lord Buddha cannot be explained in words that relate to reality or non-reality.

"Subhuti, if Enlightened Disciples, while exercising charity, entertain subjective thoughts that discriminate between themselves or other selves with the intent of helping sentient beings, are unworthy to be called Enlightened Disciples. They are like persons who walk in impenetrable darkness and see nothing, but an Enlightened Disciple, who practices charity with a mind detached from every such concept as the self, other selves, and the intent of helping sentient beings, will be like a person with sharp vision who walks in the bright light of day.

"Subhuti, in the future, any good and holy disciple, whether a man or a woman, who faithfully studies and practices this Scripture, will in attain immeasurable and endless blessing and merit in the Holy Eyes of the Lord Buddha."

The Lord Buddha asked Subhuti: "If good and holy disciples, whether men or women, in their eagerness to practice charity, were to sacrifice their lives morning, noon and night, without stopping, for an inconceivable period of time[16] equal to the number of the grains of sand in the River Ganges, would their blessing and merit be great?"

Subhuti replied: "Honored of the Worlds, it would be very great."

The Lord Buddha continued: "Subhuti, if another disciple should study and practice this Scripture with a pure faith, that disciple's blessing and merit would be greater, and if another disciple, in addition to studying and practicing this Scripture, were to enthusiastically teach it to others, copy it, and distribute it, that disciple's blessing and merit would be far greater.

---

[16] Kalpas

"Subhuti, this Scripture has a virtue and power. Its truth is infinite, its worth unsurpassed, and its merit is infinite. The Lord Buddha has delivered this Scripture only to those disciples who have entered the path that leads to the Most Supreme Enlightenment and earnestly persevere to practice the compassion of Enlightened Disciples who walk the path[17] that leads all people to salvation. The Lord Buddha recognizes and supports all disciples that strive to enthusiastically and faithfully study and practice this Scripture, teach it to others, and distribute it widely. He sustains them until they awaken to its vast, endless, and wonderful virtues. They will share the burden of compassion and the reward of the Most Supreme Enlightenment.

"The disciples who have not been able to free themselves[18] from such subjective concepts of sensual experiences as the existence of self, personality, other selves, or an eternal Universal Self are not yet able to faithfully study, practice, and explain this Scripture to others.

"Listen to me, Subhuti, wherever this Scripture is studied, practiced, and taught, that place is sacred ground to which countless immortals and celestial spirits will bring offerings. Such places, however humble, will be revered as though they were famous temples or golden pagodas. Thousands of pilgrims will come to them to worship and offer incense while thousands of immortals and angels will hover over them, sprinkling them with celestial flowers."

---

[17] Mahayana or Great Vehicle
[18] Hinayana or Lesser Vehicle

The Lord Buddha continued: "If there should be among the faithful, disciples who have not concluded the consequences of their actions[19] and must suffer the retribution of sins that they committed in previous lives by being demoted to a lower caste, by devoutly studying and practicing this Scripture, and because of that practice be despised and persecuted by others, the consequences of their actions will be immediately concluded and they will awaken to the Most Supreme Enlightenment.

"Subhuti, infinite ages ago, before the Dipankara Buddha, there were an almost endless succession of Buddhas whom I served and from whom I received instruction. My conduct was blameless and I received an abundance of blessings and merit. Yet, if in the future ages, even to the last age of the world, a disciple should study and practice the teachings of this Scripture, that disciple's blessing and merit would far exceed the poor merit I received while serving those many Buddhas. The abundance of that disciple's blessing and merit, in proportion to what I received, would be beyond comprehension.

"Subhuti, such disciples, in far off future ages, whether men or women, might become delirious, unstable in mind, and doubt what they have heard, when they attempt to comprehend the proportion of blessing and merit that they will receive. Just as the meaning of this Scripture is beyond the comprehension of ordinary people, the measure of blessing and merit that it bestows is equally beyond comprehension.

---

[19] Karma

Then Subhuti asked the Lord Buddha: "Honored of the Worlds, if good and holy disciples, whether men or women, have entered the path that leads to the Most Supreme Enlightenment and find that they are unable to keep their minds tranquil and undisturbed, how are they to completely subdue their wandering thoughts and excessive desires."

The Lord Buddha replied: "Subhuti, any good and holy disciples, whether men or women, who have begun the practice of concentrating their minds in an effort to reach the Most Supreme Enlightenment, should cling to the one thought that when they reach the Most Supreme Enlightenment, they will save all sentient beings and bring them into the eternal peace of Nirvana. If their purpose and vow is sincere, these sentient beings are already saved. However, Subhuti, you must realize the truth; not one sentient being has ever been saved, because if any Enlightened Disciple has ever kept in their mind any such subjective concepts as the existence of self, personality, other selves, or an eternal Universal Self, they could not be called Enlightened Disciples. These are subjective concepts. There are no sentient beings to be saved and there is no self that can begin the practice that leads to the Most Supreme Enlightenment."

The Lord Buddha asked Subhuti: "What do you think? When the Lord Buddha was a disciple of the Dipankara Buddha, did he receive any teaching whereby he was able to reach the Most Supreme Enlightenment?"

Subhuti replied: "No, Honored of the Worlds, because as I understand your words; when the Lord Buddha was with the Dipankara Buddha, he received no subjective concepts as a 'teaching' that would cause him to seek the Most Supreme Enlightenment."

The Lord Buddha was very pleased with Subhuti's response and said: "You are right, Subhuti. Truly there is no such subjective concept as 'teaching'. If there had been, the Dipankara Buddha would not have told me that, in some future time, I would awaken as a Buddha under the name of Sakyamuni, because, when people awaken, they realize that concepts as 'Buddha' and 'Most Supreme Enlightenment' are entirely subjective and whose essence is identical with the essence of all things—universal, unimaginable, and beyond comprehension.

"There may still be some disciples who insist that they have received some teaching from the Lord Buddha that justifies their quest for the Most Supreme Enlightenment, but in reality the Lord Buddha truly has given no one any teaching that would justify such a quest. Subhuti, the level of awakening that the Lord Buddha reached is both the same and not the same as the Most Supreme Enlightenment. This is another way of saying that the sensual experiences of all things is of the same substance as awakening and the Most Supreme Enlightenment. It is neither reality nor unreality. It rests with all sensual experiences in emptiness and in silence beyond comprehension. That is why nothing can ever be understood by any subjective concept of sensual experiences no matter how universal that concept may be. That is why a disciple can say that the Lord Buddha has taught the way that leads to the Most Supreme Enlightenment and, at the same time, there is no such teaching."

The Lord Buddha asked Subhuti again: "Subhuti, can you imagine a person having a very large physical body?

Subhuti replied: "Honored of the Worlds, surely the Lord Buddha is not speaking in terms of the largeness of a human body as a subjective concept; rather I should say that these words carry only an imaginary meaning."

The Lord Buddha continued: "Subhuti, it is the same when an Enlightened Disciple speaks of saving numberless sentient beings. If such persons were to have in mind subjective concepts as sentient beings or definite numbers of sentient beings, they are unworthy to be called Enlightened Disciples. The reason they are called Enlightened Disciples is because they have abandoned all such subjective concepts. What is true of one subjective concept is true of them all. The Lord Buddha's teachings are free from all subjective concepts as the existence of self, personality, other selves, or an eternal Universal Self.

"Moreover, if an Enlightened Disciple was to say, 'I shall create countless Buddhist Kingdoms', that disciple would be unworthy to be called an Enlightened Disciple because the Lord Buddha has clearly taught that when Enlightened Disciples use such words, they do not have any subjective concept of sensual experiences, but understand that such expressions are merely so many words.

"Subhuti, only those disciples whose understanding can enter deeply into the meaning of the Lord Buddha's teaching about the selflessness of all things, living and nonliving, and who can clearly appreciate their significance, are worthy to be called Enlightened Disciples."

The Lord Buddha asked Subhuti: "What do you think, does the Lord Buddha have a physical eye?"

Subhuti replied: "Honored of the Worlds, the Lord Buddha truly has a physical eye."

The Lord Buddha asked Subhuti: "What do you think, does the Lord Buddha have the eye of Enlightenment?"

Subhuti replied: "Honored of the Worlds, the Lord Buddha truly has the eye of Enlightenment. He would not be the Lord Buddha if he did not."

The Lord Buddha asked Subhuti: "What do you think, does the Lord Buddha have the eye of Wisdom?"

Subhuti replied: "Honored of the Worlds, the Lord Buddha truly has the eye of Wisdom."

The Lord Buddha asked Subhuti: "What do you think, does the Lord Buddha have the eye of Truth?"

Subhuti replied: "Honored of the Worlds, the Lord Buddha truly has the eye of Truth."

The Lord Buddha asked Subhuti: "What do you think, does the Lord Buddha have the eye of a Buddha's love and compassion for all sentient beings?"

Subhuti replied: "Honored of the Worlds, the Lord Buddha truly has the eye of a Buddha's love and compassion for all sentient beings."

The Lord Buddha asked Subhuti: "What do you think, did the Lord Buddha declare that there truly are grains of sand in the River Ganges?"

Subhuti replied: "Honored of the Worlds, the Lord Buddha did not declare that there truly are grains of sand in the River Ganges. You only spoke of them as grains of sand."

The Lord Buddha asked Subhuti: "What do you think? If there were as many River Ganges as there are grains of sand in the River Ganges, and if there were as many Buddhist Kingdoms as there are grains of sand in all of these rivers, would the number of these Buddhist Kingdoms be very large?"

Subhuti replied: "Honored of the Worlds, the number of these Buddhist Kingdoms would be very large."

"Subhuti, within these innumerable Buddhist Kingdoms there are innumerable forms of every species of sentient beings, all with different mental capabilities and concepts about the nature of things. The Lord Buddha knows all of these, but none of them is held in his mind as a subjective concept of sensual experiences. They are merely in his thoughts. None of these infinite stores of concepts from beginning-less time into the unending future are comprehensible."

The Lord Buddha continued: "What do you think, Subhuti: if a disciple should give alms equal to the seven treasures sufficient to fill the three thousand great worlds, would that disciple gain considerable blessing and merit?"

Subhuti replied: "Honored of the Worlds, such a disciple would gain considerable blessing and merit."

The Lord Buddha instructed Subhuti: "If there was any real substance to the concept of blessing and merit, if they were nothing more than the expression of words, the Lord Buddha would not have used the words 'blessing and merit'."

Again the Lord Buddha asked Subhuti: "Can the Lord Buddha be perceived by his perfect material body?"

Subhuti replied: "No, Honored of the Worlds, the Lord Buddha cannot be perceived by his perfect material body, because what the Lord Buddha referred to as his perfect material body is merely an expression of words and therefore meaningless."

Again the Lord Buddha asked Subhuti: "Can the Lord Buddha be perceived by any form, feeling, thought, impulse, or consciousness?"

Subhuti replied: "No, Honored of the Worlds, the Lord Buddha cannot be perceived by any of the senses, because what the Lord Buddha referred to as form, feeling, thought, impulse, or consciousness are merely expressions of words, without meaning.

Words would fail even the most advanced Enlightened Disciples if they were to describe their experience of the Lord Buddha."

The Lord Buddha gave Subhuti this warning: "Do not believe that the Lord Buddha considers that he has developed a system of teaching or dogma. You should never consider such a shameful thought. Any disciple who believes such a thing not only misunderstands the Lord Buddha's teaching but insults him as well. What I have just referred to as a system of teaching or dogma has no meaning. The truth cannot be dissected and arranged into a system. Such words are only a figure of speech."

Then the virtuous Venerable Subhuti asked the Lord Buddha: "Honored of the Worlds, in future ages, when sentient beings hear this Scripture, will they awaken to the essential elements of faith?"

The Lord Buddha scolded Subhuti: "Why do you continue to cling to such subjective concepts. There are no such things as sentient beings or non-sentient beings, because the concepts of sentient and non-sentient beings are unreal and non-existent. When the Lord Buddha uses such words in his teachings, he has used them merely as figures of speech. Your question is irrelevant."

Again Subhuti asked the Lord Buddha: "When you reached the Most Supreme Enlightenment, did you feel that nothing had been attained?"

The Lord Buddha replied: "Subhuti that is precisely the point. When I awakened to the Most Supreme Enlightenment, I did not feel anything nor grasp any subjective concept of teaching or dogma. Even the words 'the Most Supreme Enlightenment' are mere words.

"My awakening to the Most Supreme Enlightenment is exactly the same awakening as all others who have reached it. It cannot be differentiated or considered higher or lower than what others have reached. It is entirely free of any subjective concept of self, personality, other selves, or an eternal Universal Self, but embraces all acts of love, compassion, joy, and self-control.

"Subhuti, when disciples are moved to perform acts of charity they should do so by practicing the Wisdom of Mindfulness.[20] There is no subjective distinction between one's own self and the selfhood of others. Disciples practice charity not only with objective gifts but also with gifts of kindness and compassion. Any disciple who simply practices kindness and compassion will quickly awaken to the Most Supreme Enlightenment. However, the Lord Buddha does not intend that any disciple, when practicing charity, should entertain any subjective concepts of kindness and compassion because these are only words and the practice of charity is without any concept of a self who offers a gift or the other self who is the recipient.

"Subhuti, if a disciple were to gather the seven treasures into a pile as high as Mount Everest and as large as the many Mount Everests in the three thousand great universes and gave them away as an act of charity, that disciple's merit would be less than the merit of a disciple who simply studied and practiced this Scripture

---

[20] Shila Paramita

and out of kindness and compassion explained it to others. Indeed, the second disciple's blessing and merit would exceed the merit of the first by an incomprehensible degree."

The Lord Buddha continued: "Subhuti, do not think that the Lord Buddha believes within himself that he will bring salvation to all sentient beings. Do not even consider such a thought. In reality, there are no sentient beings to be saved by the Lord Buddha. Should there be any sentient beings to be saved by the Lord Buddha, it would mean that he was clinging to such subjective concepts as self, personality, other selves, or an eternal Universal Self. Even when he refers to himself, he does not cling to such a subjective concept. Only ignorant people think of selfhood as belonging to them. Subhuti, even the expression 'ignorant people' does not mean that there are actually such beings. It is only a figure of speech."

The Lord Buddha asked Subhuti: "What do you think? Can the Lord Buddha be recognized by the thirty-two signs of a great man?"

Subhuti replied: "Honored of the Worlds, the Lord Buddha may be recognized by the thirty-two signs of a great man."

The Lord Buddha corrected Subhuti, saying; "If it were possible to recognize the Lord Buddha by means of the thirty-two signs of a great man, he would be no different than one of the Great Kings[21] whose dominion embraces the entire earth. Since

---

[21] Chakravartin

these also have the thirty-two signs of a great man, they should also be called a Lord Buddha."

Subhuti realized his mistake: "Honored of the Worlds, now I realize that the Lord Buddha cannot be recognized by his thirty-two signs of a great man."

Then the Lord Buddha recited this verse:
> "A person who reveres the image of the Lord Buddha,
> Offering prayers and incense,
> And thereby claims to know him,
> Dwells in ignorance and does not know true blessedness."

The Lord Buddha continued: "Also Subhuti, do not think that the Lord Buddha awakened to the Most Supreme Enlightenment without his thirty-two signs of a great man. If you believe that, when you begin the practice that leads to the Most Supreme Enlightenment, you will believe that you should reject all scientific classifications regarding the physical world. That is a serious error. Any disciple who enters the path that leads to the Most Supreme Enlightenment should neither accept nor reject such subjective concepts."

"Subhuti, if a disciple gave away a quantity of the seven treasures equal to the amount needed to fill as many worlds as there are grains of sand in the River Ganges and if another disciple realizes the selflessness of all things and thereby awakens in perfect tranquility, the second disciple's merit would far exceed that of the first who practiced objective charity alone. Enlightened Disciples are unaffected by considerations of blessing or merit."

Subhuti asked: "Honored of the Worlds, what does all this mean?"

The Lord Buddha answered: "Enlightened Disciples do not grasp at blessing and merit as a personal possession because they are entirely unaffected by any consideration of blessing or merit."

The Lord Buddha addressed Subhuti: "If any disciple were to say that the Lord Buddha is coming or going,[22] lying down or standing, that disciple would not understand what I have been teaching because the true Lord Buddha is neither coming from anywhere nor going to any place. They are merely words."

The Lord Buddha continued: "Subhuti, if a good and holy disciple, whether a man or a woman, were to grind the three thousand great universes into the finest grains of powder and blow them into vast, empty space, would those grains of powder have individual existence?"

Subhuti replied: "Honored of the Worlds, as each grain of fine powder dissipates through infinite space, they might be said to have an individual existence, but the Lord Buddha is only using words which have no meaning. They are merely figures of speech. Matter does not have an independent and individual existence.

"Also, when the Lord Buddha refers to the three thousand great universes, he is only doing so as a figure of speech, because if the three thousand great universes really existed, there would be eternity and unity in matter. Whether as finely ground powder or

---

[22] Tathagata—He who has come and he who has gone

as great universes, there is neither unity nor eternity in matter. Such concepts are merely words."

The Lord Buddha was very pleased by his reply and said: "Subhuti, although human beings have always clung to the subjective concepts of matter and great universes, these concepts are only illusions with no basis in reality. Even the concepts of eternity and unity are unfathomable."

The Lord Buddha continued: "If a disciple were to say that the Lord Buddha, in his teachings, constantly referred to himself or other selves, or an eternal Universal Self, would that disciple have understood the meaning of what I have been teaching?"

Subhuti replied: "No, Honored of the Worlds, that disciple would not have understood the Lord Buddha's teachings, because the Lord Buddha has never referred to objects as having actual existence. He has only used words as figures of speech. All concepts of self, personality, other selves, or an eternal Universal Self are entirely unreal and illusive."

The Lord Buddha affirmed Subhuti's remarks, saying: "When disciples enter the path that leads to the Most Supreme Enlightenment, they ought to know, to understand, and to realize, that all objects and teachings have no reality and are merely subjective concepts."

The Lord Buddha continued: "Subhuti, if any disciple gave to the Lord Buddha enough of the seven treasures to fill an infinite number of worlds, and if other disciples, whether good and holy men or women, in their practice that leads to the Most Supreme

Enlightenment, should sincerely and faithfully study and practice even a single verse of this Scripture and explain it to others, their total blessing and merit would be infinitely greater.

"Subhuti, how can a disciple explain this Scripture to others without clinging to subjective concepts like objects, sensual experiences, and teachings? It can only be done by resting in perfect tranquility, dismissing all extraneous thoughts, mindful of the suchness that is the Lord Buddha. All concepts of matter and sensual experiences, and all the emotions that have been conditioned by them are like a dream, a phantasm, a bubble, a shadow, the glistening dew, and the lightening flash. All activities of the mind are like this. Faithful disciples dismiss extraneous thoughts and keep their minds in perfect tranquility."

Then Subhuti inquired of the Lord Buddha: "Honored of the Worlds, what Name shall we give to this Scripture so that we may study, understand, and reverence it?"

The Lord Buddha replied: "Subhuti, this Scripture shall be known as *The Diamond Sutra*,[23] the great Awe-inspiring Wisdom that brings faithful disciples to The Other Shore. By this name it will be revered, studied, and practiced, but when the Lord Buddha named it *The Diamond Sutra*, he did not consider it any definite or subjective concept, so that is why he gave it that name. The Scripture is hard and sharp like a diamond and cuts away all subjective concepts and brings faithful disciples to The Other Shore.

---

[23] Vajracchedika Prajna Paramita

Then Subhuti respectfully asked the Buddha: "Honored of the Worlds, in the future, when this scripture is proclaimed to those who are destined to hear it, will they awaken to true faith?"

The Lord Buddha replied: "Have no fear. Even five hundred years after the nirvana of the Lord Buddha, many disciples will observe the monastic vows and will devote themselves to charity. They will awaken to pure faith when they hear this scripture proclaimed. However, you should know that the roots of this faith were planted in many ages past by myriads of Buddhas, so that when in the future, disciples hear this scripture, their minds will instantly awaken to a pure and holy faith.

"Subhuti, the Lord Buddha can see this and is perfectly aware of all such potential disciples, and these will receive immeasurable blessing and merit, because these disciples will have abandoned such subjective concepts of sensual experiences as the existence of self, personality, other selves, or an eternal Universal Self. If they had not, their minds would unavoidably cling to such things and they would not be able to practice charity or practice a pure and holy faith.

"Also, these disciples must have abandoned all subjective ideas concerning the existence of self, personality, other selves, or an eternal Universal Self because if they have not, their minds would inevitably cling to such relative ideas. These disciples must have already abandoned all subjective ideas about the non-existence of a personal self, personality, other selves, or an eternal Universal Self. If they have not, their minds will still cling to such ideas.

Therefore, every disciple who seeks enlightenment should abandon all conceptions of self, personality, other selves, or an eternal Universal Self. They also should abandon all ideas about such conceptions and all ideas about the non-existence of such conceptions.

"While the Lord Buddha, in his teachings, makes use of words concerning conceptions and the ideas about them, enlightened disciples must keep in mind that these conceptions and ideas have no reality. These words are like a raft that is used to cross a river. The raft has no further use after the river is crossed. It is abandoned. If these subjective conceptions of things and about things are completely abandoned as one awakens to complete enlightenment, how much more should one abandon conceptions of non-existent things?"

As the venerable Subhuti listened to the words of the Lord Buddha, the teaching of the Scripture penetrated into the debts of his being and he realized the truth that leads to the Most Supreme Enlightenment. Moved to tears, he declared, "Lord Buddha, never before have I understood what you have taught by this Scripture. You have opened my eyes to this Awe-inspiring Wisdom.

"Honored of the Worlds, you have taught us that the true nature of sensual experiences is impermanent and possesses no subjective or transient meaning. This teaching is truly a raft that carries faithful disciples to the Other Shore. Honored of the Worlds, now that I have had heard this Scripture, I can easily concentrate my mind on it and clearly understand how important it is. I have awakened to a pure and holy faith. In the future, even five hundred years from now, any disciples who are ready to hear it and ready to attain enlightenment, able to concentrate on it, to realize clear understanding of it, and to awaken pure faith in it, will receive the highest admiration and praise. Such disciples will be able to awaken to a pure faith because they have ceased to cling to such subjective concepts as the existence of self, personality, other selves, or an eternal Universal Self. Any disciples who cling to such subjective concepts as to one's own self, cling to something that does not exist. In the same way, concepts of other personalities, living beings, or an eternal Universal Self are all subjective and expressions of things that do not exist. A disciple who is able to discard all subjective concepts of sensual experiences or about sensual experiences will immediately become a Buddha."

The Lord Buddha was very pleased with Subhuti, saying: "You are exactly right. If in the future, a disciple who hears this Scripture is not disturbed or frightened by its concepts, and does not hide from it, will receive the highest admiration and praise."

When the Lord Buddha finished the teaching contained in this Scripture, the Venerable Subhuti, with all the assembled monks and nuns and disciples, both men and women, and all mortals and the whole realm of spiritual beings rejoiced greatly, and with a firm faith, dedicated themselves to its practice.

May the merit of this penetrate
Into each thing in all places
So that we and every sentient being
Together can realize the Buddha's Way.

The ten directions, the three worlds, all Buddhas;
All venerable ones, Great Enlightened Disciples;
The Great Way to Wisdom.[24]

---

[24] Fueko Sutra by Soto Shu Shumucho, Tokyo.

Glossary

Anagami (Pali for "non-returning") is a partially-enlightened person who has cut off the first five chains that bind the ordinary mind. An anagami has reached the third of the four stages of enlightenment. They are not reborn into the human world after death, but into the heaven of the Pure Abodes, where only anagamis live. There they attain full enlightenment (arahant) and are free from the five fetters of belief in self, skeptical doubt, attachment to rites and rituals, sensuous craving and ill-will. They are not yet free from the five fetters of craving for material existence, craving for immaterial existence, conceit, restlessness, and ignorance. Anagamis are at an intermediate stage between sakadagamis and arahants. Arahants enjoy complete freedom from the ten fetters.

Anuttara-samyak-sambodhi can also be translated as unsurpassed perfect intelligence. Nuttara—untarnished; Sam—correct view; Myak—complete wisdom; Sambodhi—enlightened knowledge.

Aranyakas were monks, ascetics who lived as hermits in strict seclusion. Some lived in the forest and devoted themselves to the idea that the original human nature was calm, still, and passive. Others lived in cemeteries and refused to approach human settlements. A third class lived near the seashore on rocks at half tide. They thus had taken on extra vows and rejoiced in wearing rough garments and living in solitude.

Arhat (See Anagami above.) The word "*arahan*" literally means "worthy one." An alternative meaning of the word is "foe-destroyer." An arhat is regarded as the highest grade of noble person described by the Buddha. The word is used in the liturgy of Theravada Buddhism to refer to the Buddha himself as well as of his enlightened disciples: *Homage to him, the Blessed One, the Worthy One, the perfectly enlightened Buddha.* An arhat has realized the goal of nirvana. Such a person, having removed all causes for future becoming, is not reborn after biological death into any samsaric realm.

Bodhisattva is a person with enlightened existence or an enlightened-being. The various divisions of Buddhism understand the word bodhisattva in different ways, but especially in Mahayana Buddhism, it refers to a person who represents the highest Buddhist ideal, a being that compassionately refrains from entering nirvana in order to save others.

Chakravartin, "literally "whose wheels are moving", in the sense of whose chariot is rolling everywhere without obstruction". In Pali, *cakkavatti* is also interpreted as "for whom the Wheel of Dharma is turning". It is a term used in Indian religions for an ideal universal ruler, who rules ethically and benevolently over the entire world. In Buddhism three types of Chakravartins are distinguished: *cakravala chakravartin*, a ruler over all four continents postulated in ancient Indian cosmography; *dvipa chakravartin* a ruler over only one of four continents; *pradesa chakravartin*, a ruler over only part of a continent. The term is not used for any historical figure. The *chakravartin* in Buddhism came to be considered the secular counterpart of a Buddha. In general, the term applies to temporal as also to spiritual kingship and leadership, particularly in Buddhism and Jainism. In Hinduism, the term generally denotes a powerful ruler, whose dominion extends over the entire earth.

Dharma is a word that is used to translate the Chinese word *Fah* which means law. It refers to the teachings of the Buddha and Buddhist practice. Dharma is the Wisdom that leads all sentient beings to enlightenment. It is a mistake however, to think of Dharma in a legalistic term like secular or canon law. There are no sanctions imposed on a person who does not practice the Dharma. They only miss the opportunity to experience enlightenment.

Hinayana, usually translated as "lesser vehicle," refers to the purpose of the Hinayana practitioners to attain Individual Enlightenment. Sometimes it is translated as "the low vehicle," "the inferior vehicle," or "the deficient vehicle," where "vehicle" (yana) means "a way of going to enlightenment". It is a pejorative term coined by Mahayana Buddhists to denigrate their opponents. Its use in scholarly publications is controversial. There are differing views on the use and meaning of the term, both among scholars and within Buddhism.

Kalpa is a measurement of an unimaginably long period of time. In Buddhism, there are four different lengths of kalpas. A *regular* kalpa is approximately sixteen million years long, and a *small* kalpa is one thousand regular kalpas, or sixteen billion years. Further, a *medium* kalpa is three hundred twenty billion years, the equivalent of twenty small kalpas. A *great* kalpa is four medium kalpas, or 1.28 trillion years. One way to understand a kalpa is to imagine a huge empty cube at the beginning of a kalpa, approximately sixteen miles on each side. Once every one hundred years, a person inserts a tiny mustard seed into the cube. According to the Buddha, the huge cube will be filled even before the kalpa ends. Another way is to imagine a gigantic rocky mountain at the beginning of a kalpa, approximately sixteen miles on a side. A person takes a small piece of cloth and wipes the mountain once every one hundred years. According to the Buddha, the mountain will be completely depleted even before the kalpa ends.

Karma is "cause" in the chain of cause and effect and comprises the elements of "volitional activities" and "action." Any action is understood to create "seeds" in the mind that will sprout into the appropriate result when they meet with the right conditions. Most types of karmas, with good or bad results, will keep persons within the wheel of samsara, or will liberate them to nirvana. Buddhism relates karma directly to motives behind an action. Motivation usually makes the difference between "good" and "bad," but included in the motivation is also the aspect of ignorance; so a well-intended action from a deluded mind can easily be "bad" in the sense that it creates unpleasant results for the actor.

Lakkhana Sutra (or *Sutra of Marks*) describes the physical characteristics of the Buddha. The Thirty-two signs of a Great Man are said to have defined the appearance of the historical

Buddha, Siddhartha Gautama, and have been used symbolically in many of his representations. They are: (i) He has feet with a level sole--Note: "feet with level tread, / so that he places his foot evenly on the ground, / lifts it evenly, / and touches the ground evenly with the entire sole." (Lakkhana Sutra); (ii) He has the mark of a thousand-spoked wheel on the soles of his feet; (iii) He has projecting heels; (iv) He has long fingers and toes; (v) His hands and feet are soft-skinned; (vi) He has netlike lines on palms and soles; (vii) He has high raised ankles; (viii) He has taut calf muscles like an antelope; (ix) He can touch his knees with the palms of his hands without bending; (x) His sexual organs are concealed in a sheath; (xi) His skin is the color of gold; "His body is more beautiful than all the gods." (Lakkhana sutra); (xii) His skin is so fine that no dust can attach to it; (xiii) His body hairs are separate with one hair per pore; (xiv) His body hair is blue-black, the color of soot, and curls clockwise in rings; (xv) He has an upright stance like that of a Brahma; (xvi) He has the seven convexities of the flesh--Note: "the seven convex surfaces,/ on both hands, both feet, both shoulders, and his trunk." (Lakkhana Sutra); (vii) He has an immense torso, like that of a lion; (xviii)The furrow between his shoulders is filled in; (xix) The distance from hand-to-hand and head-to-toe is equal--Note: incidentally, these are also the ideal proportions according to Leonardo Da Vinci's Vitruvian Man; (xx) He has a round and smooth neck; (xxi) He has sensitive taste-buds; (xxii) His jaw is like a lion's; (xxiii) He has forty teeth--Note: The average person normally has 32 teeth; (xxiv) His teeth are evenly spaced; (xxv) His teeth are without gaps in-between; (xxvi) His teeth are quite white; (xxvii) He has a large, long tongue; (xxviii) He has a voice like a Brahma's; (xxix) He has very blue eyes--Note: "His lashes are like a cow's; his eyes are blue./ Those who know such things declare/ 'A child which such fine eyes/ will be one who's looked upon with joy./ If a layman, thus he'll be/ Pleasing to the sight of all./ If ascetic he becomes,/ Then loved as healer of folk's woes.'" (Lakkhana Sutra); (xxx) He has eyelashes like an ox; (xxxi) He has a white soft wisp of hair in the center of the brow--Note: this became the symbolic urna; (xxxii) His head is like a royal turban--Note that this denotes his cranial protrusion, visible on Buddhist iconography.

Mahayana or "great vehicle" is considered one of two major branches of Buddhism existing today, the other being Theravada. However, the normal usage in the Mahayana refers to a level of spiritual motivation and practice of the Bodhisattva who works for the Enlightenment of all sentient beings. The source of the name Mahayana is polemical and has its origin in a debate about the real teachings of the Buddha. Although the Mahayana movement claims that it was founded by the Buddha himself, the earliest mention of *Mahayana* occurs in the Lotus Sutra between the First Century BCE and the First Century CE. The earliest Mahayana scriptures probably originated during the first century CE on the Indian subcontinent, and spread to China during the second century CE. Only in the fifth century CE did Mahayana become an influential school in India. In the course of its history, Mahayana spread throughout East Asia. The main countries in which it is practiced today are China, Taiwan, Japan, Korea, and Vietnam.

Nirvana is the state of complete peace in which all desires are silenced.

Paramita means p*erfect* or *perfection.* In Buddhism, the *paramitas* refer to the perfection of certain virtues by a disciple as a way to purge the effects of karma and to help live an unobstructed life while reaching the goal of Enlightenment. Mahayana Buddhism lists the Six Perfections as: (*i*) generosity, giving of oneself; (*ii*) virtue, morality, discipline, proper conduct; (*iii*) patience, tolerance, forbearance, acceptance, endurance; (*iv*) energy, diligence, vigor, effort; (*v*) one-pointed concentration, contemplation; and (*vi*) wisdom, insight.

Prajna-paramita is considered to be the principal means to reaching enlightenment, or awakening to nirvana, through its revelation of the true nature of all things. It is a practice that contains within itself its own outcome. The Heart Sutra describes *prajna* as the supreme, highest, incomparable, unequalled, and unsurpassed wisdom.

Pure Abodes are higher planes of existence above the level that humans live. It is into these levels that anagamis are born. They may be reborn into the pure abodes several times, but they never reenter the levels of human existence.

Samsara is the cycle of death and rebirth. The karmic balance at the time of death is inherited at the time of a person's rebirth through an unlimited number of lifetimes until it is neutralized and the person reaches complete nirvana.

Scrotapatti (Apatti—one who has entered; Scrota—the stream) is a person who has taken up the task of following the Eightfold Path of Holy Conduct (right view, right thought, right speech, right action, right livelihood, right effort, right mindfulness, right concentration). Such persons have opened their eyes to the dharma. Buddhist tradition has it that they have to endure no more that seven rebirths and are guaranteed that they will not be reborn into unhappy states as an animal or in hell. They can only be reborn as a human or in heaven.

Sesshin (literally "gathering of the mind") is a period of intensive meditation or zazen in a Zen monastery, usually lasting seven days. In these retreats, Monks and lay people meditate in thirty to fifty minute periods, interrupted by short periods of relaxation for rest, meals, work, and sleep. At times the Zen master will give short presentations and conduct private meetings with the retreatants to test their understanding and resolve.

Sakradagami literally means "one who once comes." Such a person will be born only one more time into human existence.

Shila Paramita is the second of the paramitas. See above.

Tathagata (pronounced: *tāht-āhgatah*) is frequently used when the Buddha is referring to himself. It means "one who has thus gone" or "one who has thus come." The term is deliberately ambiguous, reflecting the inexpressible nature of a fully liberated human being that transcends categories of being and non-being. Thus tathagata reflects the notion of a state between being and non-being. In the scriptures instead of saying 'me' or 'myself,' Gautama Buddha says, "The tathagata is such and such..." emphasizing that as an enlightened being he has gone beyond human personality - the absence of self being a central doctrine of the Buddha's teaching.

Teisho is a Buddhist term meaning a presentation by a Zen master during a sesshin.

Vajracchedika Prajna Paramita: the sutra of perfect wisdom of the diamond that cuts through illusion.

Zazen is sitting and opening the hand of thought. The legs and hands are folded, the back straight and head erect like a pillar with eyes downcast, and one breathes mindfully from the center of gravity.

www.ingramcontent.com/pod-product-compliance
Lightning Source LLC
Chambersburg PA
CBHW051716040426
42446CB00008B/921